DON'T BE A DOORMAT
Get Out with Your Integrity Intact

MELVA ALLEN

Don't Be a Doormat
Get Out with Your Integrity Intact
by Melva Allen

Published by CreativeMe Press

Copyright © 2022 Melva Allen
All rights reserved. No portion of this book may be reproduced in any form without permission from the publisher, except as permitted by U.S. copyright law. For permissions contact: creative.me.design.2020@gmail.com

Cover by Rebca Ira-P~ Rebecacovers

Scripture quotations in this book are taken from the King James Version of the Bible, unless otherwise noted.

Unless otherwise noted, all scripture quotations in this book are taken from the King James Version of the Bible.

ISBN: 979-8-9871818-0-5

Printed in the USA
1st Edition

Dedication

I dedicate this book to all the men who have come into and are no longer in my life. You all have taught me strength, faith, and hope and have drawn me closer to my Lord and Savior. Because of my tests and trials, I have been able to help my daughters in their relationships and want better for them. I won't accept anything less for them or for myself. My son will also benefit because I will not support him being the worst part of what I've experienced in relationships. He will learn to be respectful, and I work hard to model to him how to honor a woman as long as I live.

Table of Contents

Table of Contents 4

Introduction 6

Praying For The One 10

Hidden Trauma 16

Cursing My Relationships 29

Warning Flags 39

Why Did I Allow This? 55

Don't Be A Doormat 63

God's Got This 71

God, Can I Get Some Help? 76

Exercising Wisdom 81

Love Yourself 86

Bonus Content: Look for Your Blessings 98

Introduction

I want to share with you some lessons I've learned in dating and being so eager for love that I was sometimes blinded in spite of feeling very present in the moment. What I'm sharing is not another sad dating story, but it's helpful advice applicable to any relationship, whether the relationship has consisted of being a user, taker, faker, girlfriend, associate, boyfriend, or any title or label you choose that has made you feel as though you were treated like a doormat.

To those toxic relationships where someone who has felt as though they could disrespect, dishonor, or treat you less than what you deserve, good news, God already knows and has something to say to it! I had to discover this though many bumps and bruises, tests, and trials only to be led to scriptures to discover God has a greater plan. When God took me to the scripture in Isaiah 51:21-23 which states that I should never lie down and allow someone to walk over me is when I knew that I had to have an attitude adjustment, wise up, know my worth and make a change and therefore started me on my journey of not being a doormat!

It is my hope that this book will help you to know more about yourself and identify those blind spots that you possibly haven't seen in the past. I want you to be the best version of yourself and work on who you truly are in a relationship. This work that is required to stay at the top of your game should help you avoid another breakup story.

Growing up, my mom used to frequently say *"People treat you how you allow them to treat you."* Brushing off that comment, I had to go through some things to realized just how valuable that piece of advice was.

When I was a kid living with both of my parents, unfortunately, I witnessed domestic abuse until my mother removed herself and my siblings from that situation. Since I was a little girl, those memories of her abuse never left me, so I grew up with a chip on my shoulder, confidently knowing that I would never allow a man to put his hands on me. Because of her abuse, my mother engrained in my head that jealousy was evil, so

I was never weak in that department. The first sign of a jealous person, I was instantly turned off and I immediately walked away. However, I was so focused on never being physically abused, that I didn't even consider or know for that matter, what psychological abuse (emotional or mental) was, which could have similar effects. Sometimes it's hard to see because it can start subtly and the more we accept the behavior, that weakness can be exploited. But thank God for Jesus. As you grow in your faith you gain strength throughout tests and trials. Our faith will always be tested because the bible says so, therefore you can't be surprised.

> *Dear friends, do not be surprised at the fiery ordeal that has come on you to test you, as though something strange were happening to you. [13] But rejoice inasmuch as you participate in the sufferings of Christ, so that you may be overjoyed when his glory is revealed.*
>
> *1 Peter 4:12-13*

That scripture is why I share my testimony because I have been tested in relationships and instead of being frustrated with God or thinking there was something wrong with me, it caused me to grow closer to Him. As a matter of fact, all my trials have pushed me deeper into God's Word and caused me to heal, learn and now share. Don't get me wrong, I'm still learning and will forever be learning, but God put this in my heart to share with you, because we all deserve better. It is my desire that we love ourselves enough, no matter how confident we can be at times, in those insecure times and even vulnerable times that we not allow people to treat us less than our best.

So whatever you wish that others would do to you, do also to them, for this is the Law and the Prophets.

Matthew 7:12

Praying For The One

Two are better than one; because they have a good reward for their labour.

Ecclesiastes 4:9

Do you remember when you realized that you wanted a love of your own and began to imagine what that looked like? I was a bit of a practical thinker, growing up without a father, I knew that when I got into a solid relationship that led to marriage, I didn't want to lose it or let it go. Seeing my mother raise children on her own used to really upset me because I wanted her to have a partner; someone who would help and support her, take some of the load off, and lift the heavy burdens of not just providing, but raising kids also. I knew that we could not get the best of her because she only had so much to give. With 24 hours in a day and the demands of the day, when she poured herself out, she had very little poured back into her. On weekdays after working hard at work, my mother didn't arrive home until 6:00pm after the hourlong bus ride home, knowing that she would have to cook for her kids, sought short moments to relax and then start the day all over again. It was those days I wished for her to have help. I spent a good part of my childhood hoping that if my mother just had a husband or faithful man, she would no longer have to struggle and had more to give to us and enjoy life herself. Therefore, I knew that when I grew up, kids would not be in the picture unless I was married. I knew that I would require a husband who was available physically and emotionally to assist because no one should ever have to do things alone. We weren't created that way. To me, my idea of marriage has always been one of PARTNERSHIP!

Before I ever read the bible, I understood that two people are better than one. Oddly enough, even knowing that having a partner was aways beneficial, I grew up being a very independent woman, mostly because I did not want to have to depend on a man, but how much greater it would be to have one, because in my mind, that equated to power. I imagined two forces working together, having someone to depend on and have my back. One thing I learned from an early age was that we are stronger together.

My older brother was bullied in school, and all throughout elementary, middle school, and high school for being gay or acting feminine. At first, I didn't want to get involved because people made fun of how he expressed himself and how he carried himself but regardless of his life choices, I loved my brother. I would not allow anyone in my presence to hit or hurt him without me stepping in. He had to fight every day just to walk home from school. As early as I can remember, being in 2nd grade, the both of us fought (and won) and that's how we were able to walk home in peace. This continued all the way until high school, but the physical fights lessened because they knew, that if they touched my brother, they would have to deal with the whole family. That's love and that's also partnership, we had each other's back no matter what!

That is how I understood that whether I ended up living lower, middle, or upper class, or how economically stable I was, having a partner would add to my life in ways that money couldn't. Just having someone to bounce ideas off of, socially interact with, have dates with, laugh with, and do quirky things like watching movies with has always been ideal for me.

Asking God for my partner or spouse would require me to ask myself some tough questions, it may have also required me to WAIT until I get those things worked out in myself.

When I matured into adulthood and realized that trying to find that perfect man on my own and in my own way that I kept failing miserably. I discovered that I had to ask the master, Jesus. Why wouldn't I consult the ultimate matchmaker Himself if I wanted a God-ordained relationship? Men are already absent in the church, so if you're like me, you have also wondered where are all the good men?

When I married my first husband, I liked that he loved God and was a praying man, but I also liked that he was a little "street" and from the "hood." Why, because when it came to defending me, I wanted my man to be tough. But really that sounds silly, and it is silly because a true man of God would not put you in situations where he has to be a "thug." Better yet, when he starts acting "ghetto and street" you better start praying to Jesus that the god in him will show up.

So, I realized that the street image was not the smartest request, but I also understood that I wasn't alone in my thinking, that he can be "hood and holy." How about just godly, smart, handsome, provider, loving, respectful, and all those other great qualities we desire?

So, when it came to adding God to the mix, I realized why I had not consulted him in the past. Mostly because it was going to require me to make some changes. It was going to require me to fix some things within myself. Asking God for my partner or spouse would require me to ask myself some tough questions, it may have also required me to WAIT until I get those things worked out in myself. Also praying for "the one" would require one to think about those qualities that you seek in your partner and know when to walk away when they don't possess those qualities. More importantly not to settle and make excuses for them thinking we can fix them.

Lastly, putting in the work to listen to God and not your friends is very important. Trust me, you do not want just any kind of man. If that were the case, start an online dating profile, there are plenty of them who have other motives than just being your husband. But if you are tired of wasting your time, giving up time, space, money, and vulnerability for a man to just treat you like an option and leave, then you must put in the work.

Hidden Trauma

HOW IT ALL BEGAN

I was the kind of girl who boys saw as "the cool friend" however being asked to hang out or go to a dance didn't quite happen for me in my school years. Because of this, I built up a wall and acted as though I did not ever care. I wasn't the prettiest girl in school, but not the worst either. Yes, I was that tall, skinny, no-shape-having teenager, but I never lacked confidence or self-esteem. I've always accepted who I was and was ok with it. Although I hoped that someone would find me desirable enough for me to resign from being the "tag-a-long" friend.

But my first real relationship started during my sophomore year in high school. As with any other love story, when you aren't looking or expecting it is typically when it will happen.

I was approached from a boy in school, and I remember it like it was yesterday. I happened to leave class early to retrieve something from my locker and one of the basketball players approached me. This guy Bobby who I only encountered at our basketball games and recognized him for being well known as the team's hype-man asked me did I want to go to a party. Now because this guy typically brought so much attention to himself and was the loudest basketball player on the team, we all knew that he dated an older girl who also happened to attend our school. I believe she was a senior and he was a junior. Since I was both on the cheerleading squad and band, I unfortunately could never miss him.

In his flirtatious demeanor, I knew he was running game when he asked me to a party. I instantly knew it was a bad pickup line, so I sarcastically asked who would be there and he said me and you. Wow, how original was that? Immediately confronting him, I checked him about his girlfriend, and he told me they broke up. To make this long story shorter, I said he could come by my house, but I never had any intention on him being anything more than just a friend.

However, Bobby was persistent, visiting me multiple times throughout the week, just wanting to chill with me and my girlfriends. I wasn't really interested but I told my 15-year-old self, that maybe he just wanted to have sex with me, and that's why he came to my house every single day for months. So, my immature self thought that if I had sex with him, he would leave me alone. So, I ended up at his house, in his basement messing around in the dark. I remember spitting on my hand and rubbing his private parts and Bobby thought it was my tongue and instantly ejaculated. Although I was embarrassed for him, I think he instantly fell in love. But that was the end of the road for me, I wasn't really interested in him and just wanted him to go away and leave me alone. Bobby drove me home that night and I couldn't wait to tell my older brother (who was kind of a jokester) what just transpired. My brother being the goofball that he was, made up a song about our non-sexual encounter.

Hoping that this situationship was over, Bobby was back the next day, consistent and persistent as usual. However, this time my brother has now made up a song complete with a chorus reminisce of Missy Elliot's song– One Minute Man. Not only did this reveal what I shared the night prior, but my brother proceeded to poke fun at him. I was so embarrassed for Bobby and of course mad at my brother that out of guilt I suppose I instantly went into nurturer and fixer mode. Because I felt so remorseful, I instantly felt a deep connection with Bobby, and from that day forward we were boyfriend and girlfriend.

As a couple, we showered each other with attention and confess our love for one another. Bobby and I were thick as thieves, we saw each other every day of the week, seven days a week. So, when his former girlfriend reappeared, claiming her stake, I knew it was impossible that they could have been together while we were dating, because I saw him every single day.

I'm sharing this story because what started as a beautiful high school love story started to take a turn when I began to feel smothered. I was a teenager and I saw Bobby every single day, with no breaks. He liked to spoil me and take me out often for ice cream or to just watch the planes take off at the airport. He truly loved me, and I did him, but my friends were distancing themselves from me, stating that he was around too much, and they felt that I wasn't who I used to be, nor was I not fun anymore. I felt it too because my friends and I couldn't banter like we used to. It was during this time after about a year of dating when I asked Bobby for space and he did not want to give it to me, he took it as I was attempting to break up with him. I told him, I just needed a few days apart because I felt smothered, and Bobby threatened to kill himself. After brandishing a gun and pointing it at his head, I was put in a very uncomfortable position as though my choice would be a matter of life and death, so I caved in and put the issue on hold.

Witnessing my father beat my mother as a little girl, I swore that a man would never put his hands on me, and I meant that. Whenever around any male, I'd let it be known how I would never allow that, just to make myself clear and understood and did so with Bobby. I let it be known that I was a woman who would fight back if a man put his hands on me. However, I failed to realize that there were other forms of abuse, such as emotional, spiritual, and mental abuse, I was just so focused on the physical.

I was smart enough to understand that threat from Bobby was manipulation, but my hands were tied because I loved him and didn't want him to kill himself, but I resented him for forcing me to abide by his wishes.

I tried to compromise with him multiple times for space and whenever the topic came up, he'd always put that loaded gun to his temple and repeated the words "do you want me to kill myself? Do you?" He said it so much, I honestly didn't care if he did or didn't, I was just tired of being forced to stay. If I hung out with my girlfriends, he was there. If I was with my family, he was there. He was here, there, and everywhere.

So, it got go the point when we broached the topic and he made the threat, I would say in the most sarcastic way, "if you are going to kill yourself, can you just do it at home and not ruin my life and make me suffer because of your choices?" I really felt like I didn't care, if he took his life because clearly, he didn't value it enough, I just didn't want to be traumatized by witnessing someone take their own life.

I didn't know who to talk to. Bobby was a very popular guy and well-liked and I didn't want to cause any problems. I was also afraid to tell my mother or anyone else in my family or close friends at the time because this was not a topic discussed on the news or anything. I wasn't aware of any crisis or suicide hotlines and because as a kid when we used to prank call 911 or the police, I know that they meant business if I were to call them.

One day when Bobby drove me home, I thought it was impossible for him to have his gun on him, while sitting in his car I started the conversation again and told him that I was breaking up with him because I was just tired at this point. He started his "woe is me speech" and threatened to take his life I said *"fine, go ahead and kill yourself, you're not really going to do it, because if you were, you would have done it already."*

Although he didn't have his gun, he had a knife and pulled it out and slit his wrists while we were sitting in his car arguing. I screamed and ran into my house and screaming for help. I'm looking for a towel and he drove off. At this point, I had no other choice but to tell my mother what had been happening and just as I anticipated, she made me leave him. She had always said to me while in this relationship, "Melva, you are not married, you don't have to act like a wife. Live your life, you're too young to be tied down." Of course, I felt like my mother didn't know what she was talking about, we did have some good moments, but I felt it was too complicated for her to understand. Nonetheless, she said I couldn't see him anymore and so it was official, I was off the hook and free from that relationship. I have to say that I did welcome the break, but other than the smothering, he really was my best friend and what I thought to be my soulmate.

Not too long after that incident, I recall going to a friend's house and there were some guys there. I stayed a few hours and hung out and when I stepped outside to leave, Bobby was across the street watching me and apparently had been following me. I knew he was a little crazy and that he was not going to let me go easy,

I just didn't know what to do and I wasn't filled with the holy spirit at the time.

The last straw came when I was on a date with someone else and we went to the movies to see Unforgiven with Clint Eastwood. It was right in the middle of the film that I felt a tap on my shoulder behind me. Sure enough, it was Bobby. I was so embarrassed, but I asked my date to excuse me, and Bobby and I spoke briefly in the lobby. I know I said some unkind things to him because I was mad and fed up.

A few days later, one evening while I was babysitting my next-door neighbor's kids, I heard a knock at the door. It was Bobby and he calmly asked if we could just have a conversation. I said no a few times, but he insisted, so I let him in. He wanted to rehash the conversations previously and I told him that I thought it was best that we go our separate ways. It got to a point after I put the kids down to bed that he wanted to kiss me and attempted to force himself on me. As I was fighting him off and yelling for him to stop, he pulled out his gun. I thought he was going to rape me, but instead, he said he was going to kill me and then kill himself. He grabbed me and tied me up with rope and stuck a sock in my mouth. He turned evil and started putting me down, yelling at me and stuck the gun in my mouth. He said he was crazy and no one else could have me. I wasn't a religious person, but I knew of God. My thoughts on God at that time in my life was just that He didn't like me very much. I thought maybe there was something that I did that was so bad in my past that I had to leave the earth this way. But something in me made me say to myself, if there is a God, please get me out of this, I would do better, I'm sorry for all the things I've done in my life.

Thinking back to the multiple times that Bobby threatened to kill himself, I grew numb to his threats, and he knew it, but when he actually stuck the barrel of the gun in my mouth and said, "You don't think I would kill you?" Of course, I agreed and said I thought that he would.

While Bobby was in his evil mode, I could see the darkness in his eyes and he was clearly being used by the devil, I just kept quiet while he was feeling empowered and taunting me. As he was about to put the sock back in my mouth, I mumbled and told him that I had a request. By the grace of God, I said something to the effect of *"before you kill me, can I just breath my last breath of fresh air?"* Don't ask me why I said that, but he complied. With both my hands and ankles still tied up, he untied my ankles and walked me to the door and opened the screen door while guiding and controlling my movement. As soon as I stepped foot on the porch, I found the courage to break-away and just started running and screaming. I remember running in a zig-zag pattern, so that if he shot, it wasn't a clear direction. This had to have been around 2 or 3 o'clock in the morning. Since I lived next door, my mother heard my screams. Funny that as a mom, out of a crowd or even a whisper, you can always recognize your child's cry. I screamed, *"help me, help me, somebody help me",* and my mom opened the window and yelled my name. I said *"mommy, Bobby is trying to kill me"* and my mom yelled *"I have a gun and if you hurt my daughter, I will kill you."* Bobby got in his car and took off.

It was a blur from that point for about a month, but I know the police were called and there were no charges filed. My uncle and cousins were also called, and I was told that they also took care of it, but I didn't know what that meant.

Again, I had little recollection of anything afterwards, I somehow emerged from that night and life went on. We eventually moved into a new home across town, but just so happened it was in the same housing complex as Bobby.

When I got my first job at Wendy's, Bobby ended up getting a job there too just to spite me. I had to work there because I was saving for my first car, so I didn't want to quit, but I told him that he had to leave, or I would, because he only took the job to work with me. Bobby didn't care what I thought, but when I was able to dodge his schedule and we didn't even get a chance to work together, he eventually left.

He was still very popular in school, and no one knew what happened, so he continued to live my life while I buried myself with school and work just to stay busy.

Because it was his senior year, I remember one of our last encounters was seeing him at some school dance with one of the school's most popular girls and my heart just broke. Don't know why I felt this way, but I couldn't stop crying and I called my sister because I couldn't hold it together enough to go to work. She came over and just let me cry on her lap. I told her my heart felt like it broke into a million pieces, and I wasn't sure why because I no longer wanted to be with him, but I kind of resented him for moving on like I was nothing and seeming to live his best life without having any consequences for his actions.

Cursing My Relationships

After that high school heartbreak, I swore off relationships and unknowingly allowed that trauma to impact my life for years. I remember saying to myself and making a conscious decision that I did not want to be in a relationship, I didn't want a man to love me, and I did not want to be a wife, nor have a man's child while I was young. And that was the choice and decision I made. I didn't want a relationship, I just wanted to casually date and have sex but no commitment and do things my way; and I was only 16 years old.

After that relationship I moved forward, never looking back, felt fine, felt normal, and felt like I was in control of my destiny. But little did I know at the time that I had spoken a word curse over my life and what I spoke impacted all my relationships moving forward. I was not aware that instead of affirming God and declaring His scriptures, I was actually speaking death, I was speaking anti-relationship, self-sabotage, and fear into my life, and over my future relationships as an act of pride and maybe even bitterness.

Death and life are in the power of the tongue: and they that love it shall eat the fruit thereof.

Proverbs 18:21

But those things which proceed out of the mouth come forth from the heart; and they defile the man.

Matthew 15:18

Out of ignorance, I was determined to do relationships my way or so I thought, but that did not quite work out how I thought. I said to myself, now I can really have some fun and date all kinds of men and so I did. I went out on dates with men outside my race, white, Muslim dark, light, tall, heavy, skinny, and men much older than I, you name it, I was open. I didn't realize until I was almost 30 years old, how that high school relationship and trauma impacted how I saw men.

WATCH YOUR TONGUE

Another way that I cursed relationships was by putting my mouth on them. Every little thing a man did, I complained to a friend, and of course, gossiping invites word curses. Instead of taking it to God, and praying for them and myself, I just kept the negative energy going by giving it life. I did that by rehearsing things they did and talking about the characteristics I didn't like in order to have someone agree with me. I did not realize until I started to see a pattern of relationships not working out that I'm giving the devil what he wants, to kill and destroy those relationships with my tongue. Most importantly, you don't want it done to you. Think of the betrayal you would feel if you knew that your partner was spilling all the tea or complaining to someone else about you.

Gossips reveal secrets; don't associate with those who talk too much.

Proverbs 20:19 CEB

When I realized the damage I was doing and decided to stop gossiping about men that I was dating and disclosing parts of my relationship is when I started to see a difference.

I decided to talk to God. This is a practice that you should do in any relationship is to see what God says. We can do that by simply getting alone with God in a quiet place and just talk to Him as your fried, search out some scriptures about your situation, read and pray over them and then listen to hear God.

I once dated someone and because we were introduced by a mutual friend, his friend would say things to me like, "Yeah, I talked to your boy, and I was telling him that's how women are. I told him to chill out, this is what women do...." Well at the time it went over my head because I didn't mind the friend giving him advice and trying to help him out, but at the demise of that relationship, when I prayed about it, God showed me through scripture and a dream that the man I was dating kept putting his mouth on me, gossiping about me, talking about me behind my back and complaining about me. The irony of it is that I randomly would ask him if there was anything that he didn't like about me, thought I should change or bothered him, and he always said no. So, at the end of the day, God saw what he was saying behind my back, and it was only when I took it to God that he exposed the truth of the matter.

One who seeks love conceals an offense, but one who repeats it divides friends.

Proverbs 17:9 CEB

Gossip is not just repeating what you heard or talking about someone, but it's speaking word curses and that's exactly what the devil wants because he is anti-relationship anyway. Whatever God wants, Satan wants the opposite.

Gossip can destroy relationships and cause a lot of hurt, not to mention betrayal. What we all have to realize is that for some it takes a lot to be vulnerable, transparent, and let down the walls and let another person in to see their true selves, so when you go and talk about them behind their back, it can take a while to repair even after forgiveness is given. Not to mention it can possibly damage another person's reputation.

A slanderer walks around revealing secrets, but a trustworthy person keeps a confidence.

Proverbs 11:13 CEB

Where curses are involved, the devil is lurking around like a lion seeking whom he can destroy, so that liar the devil likes to work through weak, wounded, and insecure people. When negative words are released, demonic spirits will attach themselves to those negative words ready to perform hurt and harm.

I recall during my first pregnancy I had relatives saying (with no evil intent) "Your kid is going to be just like you." Or "wait until your kids put you through the ringer." Under my breath, I would say "I rebuke that in the name of Jesus!" I never came into agreement with that word and when I was alone in my prayer time, not only did I forgive them for making the statements, but I spoke blessings over my unborn child and have done that for all my children. Whether they knew it or not, they were speaking word curses.

Let me be more specific, the curse of words includes the words we speak over ourselves and what others have spoken about us that do not align with what the Word of God says about us. That includes those microaggressions or passive-aggressive comments spoken from others that are intended to inflict harm, wish you evil or disparage you. It's what some people refer to as "hating" as well.

Think about comments you've heard throughout your life that have wounded you, those were curses. Has anyone ever said to you undeservedly "You're so clumsy . . . You'll never amount to anything . . . You'll never change . . . You're going to be just like your mother . . .You'll never find anyone to love you . . . I wish you were dead . . . I wish you'd never been born . . . You always . . . You never . . ." etc.

For many years I listened to a specific relative speak negatively about my brother, that he would be a thug, end up in jail, won't live long, etc. Repeatedly that was what was spoken over his life, and he lived up to it, always in trouble, in and out of jail and eventually murdered without even knowing what they said. Imagine if that person prayed blessings over him.

BREAKING CURSES

At that time, I wasn't familiar with how to break word curses, but now I know. You can do so in 4 simple steps:

1. Repent – before you get before God in prayer, make sure your hands, mind, heart, and spirit are clear and right with God. Repent for your sins, sins of the past, thoughts, dreams, imaginations that you've had that wasn't pleasing to God. Repent for pride, idolatry, disobeying God's commandments, and any other sins you know you are guilty of, especially unforgiveness. Forgive those whom you know have spoken a curse, pray for them and release them. God's Word says that He is faithful to forgive us of our sins.
2. Find scriptures that refute what has been spoken and write them down. It is important to know your authority in God's Word. It says He gives us power, love, and a sound mind, so use that power. Curses respond to the authority and power of Jesus. They leave when we command them to leave and take authority over them.
3. Begin to name those curses audibly and say "I break every curse off my life and every curse sent by Satan. I renounce [insert the curse(s)] in

the name of Jesus. I come out of agreement with what has been spoken over my life. I cancel every form of evil brought against me. Lord, you said in your Word [recite scripture] and You said that your Word will not return void and you are not a man that you should lie, nor the son of man that you should repent." End with pleading the blood of Jesus over you and your family members.

4. Start to praise and thank God for doing it by faith. Thank God for breaking every chain, honoring His Word, and being faithful. Just break out into a shout, dance, worship, but act as though you already have the breakthrough.

Lastly, don't forget to do a self-examination on you. You must be mindful of the impact of your words. If you yourself are cursing others, you should stop now. For instance, do you have trust issues when dating? Those insecurities will cause you to do things like look through his phone, telling him what you are not going to do, and complain about something he does, or falsely accuse. These types of behaviors only invite trouble.

Don't Be a Doormat: Get Out with Your Integrity Intact

Have you heard the saying, if you're looking for trouble, you just might find it?

Our words have the power to bless and curse. We forget that we can actually bless our partner with our words, by speaking what we desire into the atmosphere. Do you want your man to act right? Start speaking it, praying, and confessing it. Speak blessings and look for opportunities to bless, validate and encourage. Don't go through the motion of breaking curses and then turn around and be a contributor and culprit.

If you love that person and want to have a future with them, don't stop praying. Don't just pray selfish prayers for what they can do for you, but pray that God will protect them, God will take the scales off their eyes where they don't see their weaknesses or wrongs.

Life and death are in the power of the tongue.

Proverbs 28:21

Warning Flags

The thing about warning flags when you are in a relationship is that they are or were always there, but because we aren't naturally wired to be heartless or cold people, we believe in showing grace and giving people chances. I think about how God gives me grace and mercy every day, so I want to emulate that in some way as well. The bible says you never know when you are entertaining angels, so in some sense, it seems a bit complicated, because you'd hate to judge and immediately write someone off due to their imperfections, but we also know that God is not a God of confusion. But in everything, we must pray, be still and listen. With every relationship, I learn to do more of the latter two and ask God more pointed questions, such as why are they in my life, am I supposed to help them, is there something I need to receive from them, etc.

One of the things I've always said is to examine your prayers and recall what you prayed for because you when you are believing for a blessing God will send someone and so will the devil. In all my relationships in my mature years, I start praying from day one.

There has not been one relationship in that I had not seen some kind of flags, but there is truly a difference between white flags, yellow flags, and red flags and you must know the difference.

WHITE FLAGS

White flags are those relationships where things are going well, you two are connected and have expressed like or love for each other and are building a connection, but you see yourself starting to bend in order not to lose the relationship. Sometimes things are going too well, and you don't want to lose it, so you start to compromise in order to accommodate or give in to make them happy. Don't get me wrong, it could be something as simple as adapting to their lifestyle, let's say they are vegan and they expose you to that lifestyle, it could be good, no harm no foul, but if you really don't want to fully adapt to that lifestyle and you're just doing it to appease them, then that's a white flag. You step outside of your boundaries a little in order not to be seen as being difficult. Some compromise is good, but you never want to compromise yourself out of feeling good about yourself and wave the white flag to surrender. Be careful not to lose yourself in what makes the other person happy and make sure that you are getting your needs met and not justifying their needs over yours.

If you find yourself in this situation where you're slipping, you must always pray and listen to God. Ask Him for solutions and wisdom. Sometimes it's just a simple conversation or maybe a difficult one depending on the circumstance. But one thing you must hold on to is that when they started the relationship, they liked you for you and who you were. We should never try to change people but enhance or upgrade them in love. My pastor used to always say to us "Truth without love is brutality and love without truth is hypocrisy." If you can't be honest with them and let them know what makes you uncomfortable that is hypocrisy and if you just go off and are upset that's brutality, so approach with wisdom.

That is why prayer should always be at the forefront of everything you do. I would not advise you to ask God to reveal or expose things about your partner, without also asking Him for solutions, direction, and strategies. We have all heard the saying: *People are either in your life for a reason, season, or lifetime.* We don't want to be the lesson and waste our time for a reason or even a season; how draining!

I once dated a guy who liked me for me but wanted to dictate how I dressed and how to cut my hair, things of that nature. It warranted a conversation to understand his point of view and I respected some of his reasoning as a man and having to watch out for other men, but how short I should cut my hair and things of that nature, he just had to accept. That was a healthy compromise, but if he started to throw hints that he didn't want to stay if I didn't change is more along the lines of white flags.

So, if you start a relationship and see yourself approaching or suddenly in the white flag stage, I suggest you start a fast, ask God for discernment, and seek wise counsel.

> *Give your servant therefore an understanding mind to govern your people, that I may discern between good and evil, for who is able to govern this your great people?"*
>
> 1 Kings 3:9 (ESV)

YELLOW FLAGS

Yellow flags typically don't make you feel good, it's like a check in your system. But before you got to red flags, you had those yellow ones first.

We tend to notice yellow flags when we make our first excuse for them or we notice a characteristic, or flaw and feel nervous to tell them about it. Or you did tell them about something you didn't like or how something made you feel that was a little concerning and they brushed it off as if it was you, not quickly responding, apologizing, asking for clarification, or any of that.

I recall dating someone and I noticed that when I was sick, it could have been a cold, headache, any small thing, he would not call me, check in on me or if he did, he would say (the words I hate to hear) … *"I know you're tired, so I'll let you go."* I actually hate when people say that to me because if I wanted to get off the phone, I would just say so. But that is a yellow flag.

In this situation when I was sick and after like the third incident of him ignoring me during that time, I was more direct in asking him about it than I was the first two times. Essentially, he said I was tripping and that wasn't the case, although he'd done it before. I communicated to him that my feelings are real, whether he feels I'm right or wrong, they matter. I also told him what I expected and wanted to see happen in that instance and moving forward. Therefore, if he did it again, I would know that he was purposefully ignoring my feelings and refusing to respect me.

I once heard an analogy that having that check in your spirit is like your soul's check engine light. It means something is wrong and your engine needs attention and you must do something about it. Depending on the issue, it could be minor and fixable, but if you ignore it, it could get much worse, so don't ignore your feelings.

It's one thing to hope and wish a man will change, they really are not mind readers. I think it's even ok to drop hints without being passive-aggressive, but if they just don't get it, say it. But say it in love, not in a way of tearing them down. Give them some grace because they may not have experienced that with someone else. In the instance where I was ignored for being sick, I thought to myself, how bad I felt for those women before me who may not have received the support they needed because he truly didn't know what to do and the other people didn't have the courage to speak up. But in that situation, he ended up showing improvement, so I let that flag go.

But it's instances like this where you notice how they handle something and either you can communicate and move on, or you sweep it under the rug until it gets worse.

I also had a situation where I dated someone, and he would completely shut down and not communicate. He would give me the silent treatment. When he did that, I instantly felt punished, rejected, controlled, hated. So many emotions came up for me and no one had ever done that to me. When confronted, he said he did not know how to communicate (although he worked in sales and had to network and communicate for a living). It made no sense to me, but again, I told him what I needed and how it made me feel. He said he would work and even pray on it, but in the end, he didn't or couldn't and because I didn't like how it made me feel, I could no longer continue in that relationship.

Again, those yellow flags are just the beginning to getting to that major "Red Flag" and on the onset of a yellow flag, the goal is to address it immediately, but in a respectful manner. Again, never do the passive-aggressive thing. We as women tend to do that at times, we want men to read our minds and just know when they've messed up, but most of the times, they aren't thinking about it because they are not wired that way.

Remember the quote I said my mom used to say, which is borrowed from Dr. Maya Angelou that says, *"People treat you how you allow them to treat you."* But it means that I am responsible for how someone treats me because I can either allow it or not.

Keep in mind, these warning flags are not sequential, they can go from:

> White – Yellow
>
> Yellow – White
>
> Yellow – Red

It really varies, but the question is will you be prepared to when they present themselves?

RED FLAGS

Red flags are the most critical because these are the ones where you can have the most regret if not addressed. The mere definition for a red flag is a warning or a cause for concern and it's a metaphor for something signaling a problem. Instead of a check engine light, this is the blinking light saying pull over, immediate attention is required. How will you know for sure it's a red flag? You will always feel a check in your spirit. That check can feel like that still small voice, it could be the feeling in the pit of your stomach, a queasy or uneasy feeling or it could be a chill that goes up your spine. You may have just ignored it, but when you get any of these feelings while or after an encounter, you need to start paying attention because there is a problem. God gave us the Holy Spirit so that we can have this gift and use it.

My people are destroyed for lack of knowledge: because thou hast rejected knowledge, I will also reject thee, that thou shalt be no priest to me: seeing thou hast forgotten the law of thy God, I will also forget thy children.

Hosea 4:6

I once dated someone who was very mean to his ex-wife. He spoke down to her, and was controlling, rude, and aggressive toward her. When I witnessed it, I immediately addressed him about how I felt about it because it bothered my spirit. I felt that red flag pop up. In a conversation with him, I told him that I would not stand for that behavior while we were together and encouraged him to apologize to his ex-wife, forgive her and let go of the anger and bitterness and he said he would work on it. Well, when we had disagreements, guess what, I was treated the same way he treated his ex-wife. Why did I think he would treat me differently?

Now in this case, I addressed it immediately, so using the car analogy, when the warning light came on, I addressed it. However, when the light started blinking, I had to pull over, stop and address immediately, because I'm not a doormat!

Red flags can be very subtle, or it could be a glaring issue. However, it's time to walk away when it turns into abuse, and I mean any form of abuse. If you leave when you first start to notice it, you can keep your integrity intact by standing up for YOU! Choose you first. You must understand that abuse can be physical, mental, emotional, or even spiritual. ALL ABUSE IS BAD!

FORMS OF ABUSE

Manipulation, control, silence, yelling, swearing, rejection, gaslighting and anger are just a few examples of emotional abuse. I will give a man one chance because I will tell him how what they said or did makes me feel and if they do it again, then I know that they are cruel and intentional.

The one thing I can say for sure when it comes to cautionary flags is beware of a narcissist. They are your worst nightmare, you will find yourself either hurt or settling with them, and know that if you settle, you will never be your true self and fully happy because you will have to stuff down your true feelings to protect theirs.

The dictionary defines a narcissist as a person who has an excessive interest in or admiration of themselves. Narcissists are people who think the world revolves around them.

> *For I say, through the grace given unto me, to every man that is among you, not to think of himself more highly than he ought to think; but to think soberly, according as God hath dealt to every man the measure of faith.*
>
> *Romans 12:3*

Narcissism was once diagnosed as a personality disorder, referenced as a person who has an inflated sense of self-importance. This personality type makes it impossible to have a healthy relationship because narcissists are never wrong, and unable to accept criticism. It's hard for them to apologize, they blame others for their failures, they are self-righteous, know-it-alls, like to shine, and listen to no one…You get where I'm going. At first, we often mistake it for confidence, but a confident person can take constructive feedback. A narcissist will try to prove you wrong every time or reflect it on you. They tend to like to always be in control and when they are not, they will act out in some way, shape or form. Watch for this type. They are masters at switching the topic, make up a lie and then believe it. They will accuse you of judging them when you haven't, they'll turn the tables on you where you end up feeling guilty and you didn't do anything. At first you may feel like your misunderstood or going crazy, but it's not you. They are also masters at deflection, avoiding and accountability. They will rarely apologize and more importantly, they lack empathy, absolutely no empathy, controlling, selfish, petty, and vindictive. When you start to sniff them out, that is when the real problems can begin, because they are pretending to be something they are not. Be careful and don't engage because you will not win, because it's a spirit. Never do tit for tat, it's worth repeating…DO

NOT ENGAGE, let God deal with them. At this point, you know that you are not wresting with flesh and blood according to Ephesians 6. Protect your heart because they are always the victim and will seek to win at any cost, even hitting below the belt to protect their ego.

What I've learned is that the toxic person that you saw in them is how they really are regardless of if they apologize and say they won't do it again. Please know that was God exposing them. God is trying to save you. Sometimes the rejection is for your protection.

If you are a crier, watch the narcissist's reaction toward you. You will see it's like they almost have an empty stare as they watch you cry and question yourself. Once you notice this type, I would suggest running away if they do not immediately get help or counseling. It's not worth your peace.

I suggest counseling because if you read up on this type of personality, you will find that narcissists tend to be weak, wounded, broken people who refuse to allow themselves to be hurt again, so they take on this persona and convince themselves they are so great. They refuse to feel shame, guilt, or unworthiness. They usually have wounds that they don't want to deal with that could be stemming from childhood, abuse or having their heart broken.

In a spiritual sense, this is known as a spirit of pride or Leviathan. In order for them to get rid of that prideful spirit they have to fully forgive those who hurt them and let it go and most of the time, they need wise counsel to help them through it. Don't get me wrong, narcissists aren't bad people, they just have undealt trauma, and trust me, I can tell you from experience, you cannot love someone well or back to health. All you can do is pray for them, release them to God and protect yourself because they are operating in their free will and none of that is from God.

Again, the man could be a nice person, well-liked (most narcissists are), have a good heart, and more importantly doesn't fit the profile, however, don't let those superficial things hold you back from a life of happiness.

It's important to research these things that I am talking to you about so that you are well prepared. Just as if you were studying for a test, license, certification, degree, you name it, you should also put in the same effort for your relationship. You should never take advice from a song or television show. You have to be ready so that you can put on your full armor.

Put on the whole armor of God, that you may be able to stand against the schemes of the devil.

Ephesians 6:11 (ESV)

Why Did I Allow This?

Women are truly different from men. Men tend to be problem solvers, they want to fix the situation, they want to be needed, they want to feel like the king, they want respect. Now us women, we want to be loved, complemented, provided for (not just financially), nurtured, heard, and listened to. We are mostly similar in what we want from men, but what I discovered about myself is that I was trying to prove something. I wanted to prove that I would not be what you experienced in the past, so when I started dating, one of the first and natural questions I ask the person, is "why are you single?" I ask for a few reasons, first to see if you will solely blame your ex, or will you be accountable for your action in the failure of the relationship. Are you over the other person, are you bitter, or unforgiving, do you attract crazy women, are you a private person, are you remorseful, were you serious. So many things that question reveals, however internally I'm listening for why you chose me and how I am different from the previous person.

THE FIXER

I discovered that I wanted men to feel like when they were with me, they had an upgrade, like they don't have to worry about me being like the previous person, therefore I was sizing myself up to what they had in the past and didn't even really realize it.

I remember when I realized that I was doing this. I had a situation happen when I met a guy and he told me that in his previous relationship, his ex-girlfriend was verbally abusive and had been for the past 17 years. All I remember thinking was "oh, he doesn't have to worry about that with me because one, I don't even swear and two, I don't even disrespect men that way, I would never emasculate a man, so he had no worries." But then I noticed that I took on this attitude that I was better than who he previously had and expected him to be grateful and thankful.

Another man told me about their ex, their flaws, and what they no longer wanted and internally I stuck my chest out and said to myself "that's not me and thought they will really appreciate me because I'm far from that." Well, that never worked well for me. I've actually found that because I didn't know the entire story, history is bound to repeat itself. Men do this as well. When they hear about your ex, they will either feel more macho or seek to impress you in ways that your ex did not. They are or shall I say, we all are competing with the person in the past.

But as I noticed this pattern in relationships, I discovered that I am a "fixer." I wanted to fix and make better what he previously experienced and then he would treat me twice as nice, and he'd see me as the prize. But that was not ever the case.

I met this guy who ended up in the friend zone with me because all he talked about was what he did for his ex-girlfriend and how ungrateful she was. The shopping sprees, yachts trips, fancy dinners, and social outings, is what she got to experience, however, because he was burned in that relationship, I was left with the broken, abused leftover and the rebound chick. It dawned on me then that I would never get what the other woman had or experienced because she did so much damage that he had to repair, rebuild, and start from scratch.

I found that the next few relationships were very similar as though I was attracting men who were broken and once were good men at some point to other women and here, I come, nurse Melva, nursing the injured, but never receiving the "whole" person. I do believe they appreciated me, but they just didn't have it in them to give me 100%, so I accepted what they gave me. I poured into them kindness, thoughtfulness, and many other great qualities for so many years and when I look back, I realize that I gave away so much good loving and my effort was not matched and the love I gave was never reciprocated to the level in which I gave. But why is that? Because I as a woman, I'm a nurturer, I'm a comforter, I'm the partner, I'm the helper. I did not realize that men do not need or want help, they just want support. Men want to try and do things on their own and not have you judge them; they want to be recognized when they do something right and special…that's it.

> *For my fixers out there, we have to stop thinking we can show men we are better than their exes.*

It helps to ask a man what they want, instead of assuming. When I was married, it met a lot to my husband for me to thank him for taking out the trash. Initially I thought, well he doesn't thank me for washing the dishes and although I didn't need him to say that I did want him to be thoughtful when using excessive amounts of dishes. I ended up not bend to thanking him for taking out the garbage, but though counseling, maturity and learning which battles to fight, that small gesture would have gone the distance with him.

As women, we must take a step back and realize what won the man over in the first place and be consistent with that. Once we get our man and they appreciate us, just continue to be you, not what you think they want or need.

THE FREAK

I used to think that when I slept with a man, that they all wanted a freak in the bed, but boy was I wrong. First off, for some men that can be intimidating, so that won't work, not to mention, being freaky won't ever keep a man. But you have to meet them where they are at. They may have not ever experienced sex on higher levels as you may. When it comes to sex, I tend to ask little questions to see what they like and are willing to try versus putting it all out there because it's off putting to some men. For some men, if they are macho and want to have control in the bed, then your tricks and skillset will never work. It is my personal belief that when it comes to making love for men, it's like a good meal, an expensive meal 5-star meal. They will love it, even think about it the next day, savor it in that moment, but then the next day or day after they want take-out, they've forgotten how good that expensive meal was. What I'm trying to say is, although men like sex, they won't stay just for it. We as women have to stop thinking that sex will keep a man because although they love it and will jump through some hoops to get it, once they have it, it's so easy for them to walk away and forget about it so fast, like it's a passing memory.

LOOK IN THE MIRROR

I challenge you to dig deep and be honest with yourself. Look over your past relationships that weren't successful, what can you admit that you did and can do differently? When I identified that I needed to stop "proving" myself to men. I understand that I can't fix a man and that I do not want a refurbished man, but a man who is whole, healed and can give me his whole self. I stop discounting myself and cheapening my worth like I'm purchasing an open box item at Best Buy when I can afford a brand-new item. When I received this revelation, and stopped trying to prove and fix, it was like a weight fall off me. I felt the chains break. I'm more mindful and work to change my ways.

For instance, I've learned to no longer whip out my credit card when we go out to dinner on a date, thinking that they had the last one, so I'll get this one. I didn't understand how that made a man feel if I picked up the check. Now don't get me wrong, some men will allow you to do that all the time and if so, that's a major red flag. But I again wanted to show a man that I have my own money (without saying it) and that you don't have to do everything because I'm your partner, however, they aren't truly your partner until they officially make a commitment, by way of asking you to be their women or wife.

If you don't take the lessons from previous relationships, you are destined to repeat them. In every test and trial, we ought to look at what could we learn from it so that we can try to improve and not repeat the same situation.

Beloved, do not think it strange concerning the fiery trial which is to try you, as though some strange thing happened to you.

1 Peter 4:12 NKJV

As women, we must stop trying to change men. What you see is what you get. I used to think that I could love someone better, but no. If someone is not well mentally or emotionally, they need counseling and time to rest. Hurt men or women should not jump out of one relationship into another, that's why we have to really listen and ask good questions and be a junior detective.

Don't Be A Doormat

> *Therefore please hear this, you afflicted, And drunk but not with wine.* [22] *Thus says your Lord, The Lord and your God, Who pleads the cause of His people: "See, I have taken out of your hand The cup of trembling, The dregs of the cup of My fury;* [23] *You shall no longer drink it. But I will put it into the hand of those who afflict you, Who have said to you, 'Lie down, that we may walk over you.' And you have laid your body like the ground, And as the street, for those who walk over."*
>
> *Isaiah 51:21-23 (NKJV)*

When I read this scripture, in the spirit I gave God a high-five. When you know that God has your back, when you know that God is your defense and you can go to his word and the advice is just better than what your closest friend can give. I have to tell you these scriptures definitely boosted my spirit and it's the best advice ever. DON'T BE A DOORMAT!

Let's dissect what the bible says, and I will put in my own words how it spoke to me starting with verse 21. Those hurting, please hear this. I took your pain and trembling and I'm not mad at you. But I will put that same pain, hurt and trembling into the hands of your enemies, those who hurt you and those who treated you like a doormat. Those who played you, those who treated you like an option, those who overlooked you, those who took advantage of you, and you let them! That was deep.

This scripture became so plain to me after a breakup. I was in the midst of forgiving and healing and the Lord led me to this scripture. This just reminded me that not only that I deserved better, but if we just "let go and let God", He will do it. We get mad and are brought to tears for how we let people treat us, especially when we finally realize it. You can be like "oh, snap" I didn't expect it to make me feel that way, but you end up feeling like trash and more so because you let people do that to you. This applies in so many areas of life. In a breakup, at work, in your friend circles (frenemies) aka fake friends, users, haters, anyone who has played you, manipulated you, or made you feel less than your best. Anyone can walk over you, however if we just pray God's word, and give it to Him, he already said that he would take care of it.

> *And Jabez called on the God of Israel saying, "Oh, that You would bless me indeed, and enlarge my territory, that Your hand would be with me, and that You would keep me from evil, that I may not cause pain!" So God granted him what he requested.*
>
> *1 Chronicles 4:10 (NKJV)*

God saw how they treated you, and He already has a plan to deal with them for when they do it. AND HE WILL DO IT! You don't even have to confront them, because it's not like they are going to say "yeah, you got me, I'm caught." They actually are justified if they say, *"You let me, so I took advantage."* Which means that we have to have some accountability, but just know that God has already validated you and told you that you don't have to be treated like that. You are not a doormat. I'd like for you to repeat after me. I AM NOT A DOORMAT!!!

For my brothers and sisters out there, who have come to the realization that they were played and find this scripture to be as helpful and valuable as I have, there's more. But before I get to it, I just want to say that it's so refreshing that God can be your best friend and will come to your defense. He will get so mad that He's like "look, I see that you're hurt and I'm willing to take the pain you are feeling and put it on those who caused this." But it gets even better.

Awake, awake! Put on your strength, O Zion; Put on your beautiful garments, O Jerusalem, the holy city! For the uncircumcised and the unclean Shall no longer come to you. ² Shake yourself from the dust, arise; Sit down, O Jerusalem! Loose yourself from the bonds of your neck, O captive daughter of Zion! ³ For thus says the Lord: "You have sold yourselves for nothing, And you shall be redeemed without money."

Isaiah 52: 1-3 (NKJV)

God's encouragement is the greatest news. He says *"wake up and put on strength and put on your best clothes. Go and stick your chest out because those unclean people will no longer come to you."* That means, when you put on that confidence, when you get that air about you, they won't go there. They only did it because they saw a weakness in you, something they could exploit or take advantage of. However, that could have simply been us being vulnerable or desperate. Have you ever been desperate for love, for a good friend, for something to do because you were lonely for physical touch, conversation, or someone to hold you? We all have and when we did, if it wasn't the right person, they saw that vulnerability and took advantage of it. And if we can be honest, sometimes we let them to avoid the feelings of not having those things in which we craved.

SHAKE THE DUST OFF

I recall being at a low point in my life when I just wanted some attention, any attention, I wanted to be held and that caused me to make some unwise decisions and choices and I was so upset with myself when I allowed myself to be taken advantage of.

Verse 2 from Isaiah 52 says "loose yourself from the bonds of your neck or shake the dust off of your shoulder." Imagine yourself flicking the dust off your shoulders and just letting it go. It reminds me of a scripture in Matthew chapter 10 when Jesus was instructing the disciples, gave them power, and told him to go out and heal all kinds of sickness and disease. Jesus told them where to go and where not to go, but more importantly, he told them to go to the lost sheep and preach the kingdom. These two versus below made it so clear to me that if you are not worthy or welcome, take your peace back and move on!

> *If the household is worthy, let your peace come upon it. But if it is not worthy, let your peace return to you. [14] And whoever will not receive you nor hear your words, when you depart from that house or city, shake off the dust from your feet.*
>
> *Matthew 10: 13-14*

SHAKE THE DUST OFF OF YOUR FEET! Wow, if you have ever felt like are not wanted, do as the bible says…leave and take your peace with you. I can't tell you how empowered I was just after reading that. God is not playing with us, He truly is trying to help us get in order, get ready and be prepared.

Forget the former things; do not dwell on the past.

Isaiah 43:19 (NIV)

Let go, don't dwell on the past, be empowered and know that you deserve better, you deserve respect, you deserve for people to accept you for you and if you are not wanted, appreciated, or valued then walk away, don't be a doormat.

Stay away from takers. Desire to have someone who is a giver, a cyclical relationship; someone to match your efforts. If you are ever in a situation where you feel drained at the end of the day or you don't feel your best self, first separate yourself, pray for that person and ask God for discernment to know if this is the person for you. God will reveal it, but you also have to ask to be sensitive to hear God's voice, however He will speak to you. God can be attempting to communicate to you through a song, person, or the Bible. Ask God to open your senses and give you eyes to see and ears to hear the Lord and He will make it loud and clear, but then you have to be willing and brave enough to let it go and walk away.

That part won't be easy. Afterwards you will have to specifically pray for strength and ask God to fill whatever void the person you are leaving was filling because it may not be easy or feel good.

The Spirit you received does not make you slaves, so that you live in fear again; rather, the Spirit you received brought about your adoption to sonship. And by him we cry, "Abba, Father."

Romans 8:15 (NIV)

God's Got This

Let no one deceive you with empty words, for because of these things the wrath of God comes upon the sons of disobedience. ⁷ Therefore do not be partakers with them. ⁸ For you were once darkness, but now you are light in the Lord. Walk as children of light ⁹ (for the Spirit is in all goodness, righteousness, and truth), find out what is acceptable to the Lord ¹⁰ and have no fellowship with the unfruitful works of darkness, but rather expose them. ¹⁴Therefore He says: "Awake you who sleep, Arise from the dead, And Christ will give you light."

Ephesians 5:6 -10,14 (NKJV)

This powerful scripture in Ephesians 5:6-10,14 is one to meditate on in your reflection time. So many nuggets. Look at what it says.

1. Don't let that man deceive you with empty words. Don't let them play you and deceive you and if they did, God will deal with them. But here is the kicker…don't go back! BAM!

2. Don't go back to that man or any like him, because God brought you out of darkness, and now you are light. God rescued you from your Egypt, so don't go back to that bad place.
3. Walk in the light as in don't interact with those in darkness. Walk in goodness, be whole and don't go back to what was toxic, don't return to someone who hurt you. If you were walking in a relationship with a blindfold on, you are now free, don't put those blinders back on and enjoy the peace, grace, and mercy of God.

If you couldn't discern that whole scripture, you should read it 5-10 more times and sit quietly, pray, and listen to God because it's powerful.

> *If God is saying don't go back, then you shouldn't.*

When you find yourself making excuses, justifying bad behavior, or accepting less than what you deserve, remember that God delivered you. If you are wrestling with this piece of advice, I would recommend repenting, releasing, and moving forward in the Lord. He said in His Spirit, you will receive goodness, righteousness, and truth.

And as for any of your exes, pray for them. Take your mouth off them and let God deal with them. Even if they hurt you, ask God for healing and release it unto God and pray for their healing as well.

I received a revelation while reading the book of Joshua chapter 5 verses 7-9. You'll see that Joshua the son of Nun, Moses' servant, when Moses died, he was anointed to move the Israelites forward to their promised land and after they crossed the Red Sea the Lord instructed him to circumcise the male children who had been on the journey and allowed them time to heal. Once they healed the Lord said, now their reproach has been rolled away from them and they could now call that land Gilgal.

The revelation that came to me is when the Lord delivers you out of Egypt (your bad, unhealthy, undeserving relationship) then your heart must be circumcised (cut away and being made different.)

Circumcision is painful, but when the bible says they had time to heal, that showed that God gave them divine protection and covering during that time, as they were in the enemy's camp and were vulnerable and having time to heal in peace was not typical. But because the men submitted to being circumcised, the disgrace had been rolled away and they were finally free. You asked free from what? Because the Israelites were slaves for so long, they longed to return to Egypt because that was all they knew, and they felt safe in that dysfunction. So be free from being a slave or enslaved to something or someone. If you are familiar with the 5 stages of grief; there is denial, anger, bargaining, depression and then acceptance. They are all hard stages, but in the bargaining phase, you can get to a place where you want the pain to stop, and you consider going back. You rationalize why you left and start to consider taking them back, but the devil is a liar! Know that it's the trick of the enemy, but if you hold on, you will get to the acceptance phase.

I would suggest praying for healing. Ask God to circumcise your heart from that person and roll away the disgrace from that relationship. Know that it will be painful, it will hurt, you will go through those stages where you long to go back when the journey seems long, when you find yourself in the wilderness, when you feel different, just know that you are going through the painful circumcision which is a sign of the covenant that God made with Abraham and God is a covenant keeping God. While you heal, God will give you divine protection and covering. Don't try to leave that covering too quickly, remember God's got you. Don't allow yourself to be lured back in. Once you heal, this new place, this rebirth will be your Gilgal.

God, Can I Get Some Help?

There comes a time when you have to make those tough decisions to get out. You've had enough red flags but really how many does it take? Do you recall when you were at the end of a thing, and you looked back and realized that you saw the signs all along? We tend to make excuses that it's ok, I can let that one slide, I'm not perfect, so why should I expect that of them (a common one that I use). We can justify anything, plus I tend to not want to be the one who gives up too quickly on people.

The first person I dated post-divorce he presented himself well and seemed like he was what I wanted in a relationship, so continued to get to know each other. About three months into the relationship, he randomly told me that he would be busy the entire weekend and that Sunday evening, he admitted to me his weekend consisted of him moving. Now, I had never been to his house at this point because he lived a distance away. I knew he had a house because we video chatted while in his house and he sent pictures and did a video tour, but to my surprise all of a sudden he moved. He started the conversation by telling me we needed to talk. He told me that his house was foreclosed, and he had to get out and move in with his mother. He blamed this change in circumstances due to an increase in his expenses due to child support. His approach in telling me the story was that if I wanted to leave the relationship, he would understand, and gave me an out. He said he completely understood if I no longer wanted to pursue this relationship. Lastly, he presented a game plan to move back into his mom's house and save up for a few months and get an apartment. I sensed the level of shame and vulnerability in telling me that story, so I asked for some time to think about it. I actually don't recall praying about it, but I rationalized it. I said to myself, what if that was me, would I want someone to bail on me because I'm going through a hard time? So, I went with my heart posture and not God's posture. I just wanted to exercise the golden rule which is *"do unto others as you would have them do unto you."*

> *My excitement for a new relationship blinded me to the additional questions that I should have asked. That's why you can't leave out God.*

I was so busy thinking that his problem was "fixable", and that this was a temporary problem even when he doubted himself.

This is not the first time I did this. The gentleman I dated after him was a man prominent in his field of work. He made good money, solid career, and degreed, and loved God, but after about 6 months into our relationship, he lost his job. This again is what I saw as a "temporary" problem because I felt confident that he was able to just find another job and keep it moving, but he didn't feel that way. Although I sought to motivate him and not put so much pressure on him regarding dating, I see I did it all wrong.

> *Beloved, do not believe every spirit, but test the spirits to see whether they are from God, for many false prophets have gone out into the world.*
>
> *1 John 4:1 (ESV)*

Looking back on both of those situations I can tell you that making such a decision to nurture them early in a relationship was not effective for either situation. Because I didn't want to be knit picky or a diva, I let some things slide, which I'm sure we all have. I approached every potential relationship as a partnership because of course that's what the bible says in Ecclesiastes, yet where the mistake happened is that I had no ring on my finger.

> *Two are better than one; because they have a good reward for their labour. ^{10} For if they fall, the one will lift up his fellow: but woe to him that is alone when he falleth; for he hath not another to help him up. ^{11} Again, if two lie together, then they have heat: but how can one be warm alone? ^{12} And if one prevail against him, two shall withstand him; and a threefold cord is not quickly broken.*
>
> *Ecclesiastes 4:9-12 (KJV)*

Also, I did not heed the advice that my mother gave me at the tender age of 16 years old when dating, she simply said, *Melva, you're not a wife, so you don't have to act like it.* And that is a principle that all women dating should notate. However, I was so focused on wanting to give a man a preview of what they could get as a wife, that I fell into that role. I was showing them that I am responsible, I can cook, I'm a planner, I'm supportive, all that good stuff instead of focusing on enjoying the relationship. Instead of giving them something to look forward to, I was trying to impress them.

So, when looking at that scripture in Ecclesiastes 4, exercise discernment when referencing. The word with no discernment and understanding can lead to foolishness.

Behold, I am sending you out as sheep in the midst of wolves, so be wise as serpents and innocent as doves.

Matthew 10: 16 (ESV)

Exercising Wisdom

If any of you lacks wisdom let him ask God, who gives generously to all without reproach, and it will be given him.

James 1:5 (ESV)

Do not judge by appearances, but judge with right judgment.

John 7:4 (ESV)

But test everything; hold fast what is good.

1 Thessalonians 5:21 (ESV)

When you start dating, immediately and I mean immediately go on a fast. If you are not the fasting type, yet dating to be married, it's worth it to make that investment for yourself and it cannot be a one-time thing, but a weekly or monthly practice.

Some men will go right for dating for marriage and others will start off testing the water. We are praying for dating with a purpose first because it doesn't take a man years to know if you are wife material and if you hear otherwise, either they just don't know or they are buying time.

Ladies beware of excuses period. We often make the mistake on just waiting to see what the man is going to do and not let them know our standards for dating. Who told you that you should be a long-term girlfriend? Dating for more than 1-2 years without a proposal is unacceptable. Actually, two years is too long, because if we are trying to do things right according to God's way, there is really no excuse for needing to wait if you believe that God will supply all of your needs.

He who finds a wife finds a good thing, And obtains favor from the Lord.

Proverbs 18:22 (NKJV)

The bible says that when you get married, God will give you both favor. If you both are living separately and are "waiting" for a better financial situation, God can provide, but you have to make the commitment first. If you are waiting to find out more about that person, you will be doing that for the entirety of knowing that person. Again, there is no good excuse to date someone for years as a believer in Christ. If it's because of money, living arrangements, education, or employment, what does God say about it? There is really nothing that God can't provide as He says in His word in Proverbs 18:22, God will favor you and I'll take God's favor any day. But God gives favor once that commitment is made, and He will supply those needs. Whatever the barrier is that we place on ourselves that prevents us from moving forward, the bible says:

> *If ye be willing and obedient, ye shall eat the good of the land:* [20] *But if ye refuse and rebel, ye shall be devoured with the sword: for the mouth of the Lord hath spoken it.*
>
> *Isaiah 1:19-20*

So, you must be WILLING and OBEDIENT.

My goal is to get to "guilt free" sex. I don't want to have to repent after having sex as an unmarried woman because I was battling temptation.

You can only have so many dates where you are going out, holding hands, kissing, and staring into each other's eyes, and not feel tempted. These are all intimate acts and require a lot of restraint to fight off your flesh.

> *I say therefore to the unmarried and widows, it is good for them if they abide even as I.* ⁹ *But if they cannot contain, let them marry: for it is better to marry than to burn.*
>
> *1 Corinthians 7:8-9*

So, when you are in a relationship and your partner wants to get to know you more, get to know you better, just know what the bible says and that it shouldn't take years. Also, it shouldn't take you giving into having sex while they contemplate if they want to stay with you. Let me repeat, IT SHOULDN'T TAKE YEARS!

Unfortunately, we don't hear enough stories of people who met, prayed about it, and got married within months and are still together 20 + years later. We tend to hear what I believe are immature people who say things like, "we married too early or too young." So, what, you can grow together and with wise council and hard work, you can make it.

I got married in my twenties and I had enough foundation to make it work, but we both had to be willing to put in the work.

My pastor has always taught us that love is a choice. You don't "fall in love" because you can "fall out of love." You have to make a decision that you're going to love that person. You have to choose to fight for that relationship and accept that person for their flaws and seek to understand them better. We as a society will work hard and make commitments to other people such as pleasing a boss, customers, and even children. We tend to extend a longer rope of forgiveness in those instances but when they get into a relationship, suddenly there is a memory lapse. So, put in the work and be with someone who will as well. Don't compromise your morals and stick to your guns and God will bless you and give you strength and courage.

> *Do not be conformed to this world, but be transformed by the renewal of your mind, that by testing you may discern what is the will of God, what is good and acceptable and perfect.*
>
> *Romans 12: 2 (ESV)*

Love Yourself

We all have our weak moments, but we really must get to a point when we choose ourselves more than a person who is playing with our emotions.

It's already not easy to stay celibate and resist sex while waiting for the commitment that you are looking for, but another struggle is fighting and losing the battle of temptation. If you are with the one whom you feel may be "the one" and you add sex to the mix, that only leads to sin. Then you will have to find yourself repenting and if not, most likely you are avoiding praying to God because you know you messed up.

Now we all are sinners and God doesn't measure one sin greater than the other, however, if you tell God, you won't do it again, but we do, it grieves the Holy Spirit and at some point, your grace could run out. We don't know because we are not God, but if you don't turn from your sin, it's not true repentance and you are playing with God's grace.

My personal fear of having sex before marriage is twofold. First, I fear that God will not answer my prayers. I heard a pastor give an analogy of sin when I was a little girl and he said to think of a funnel from our mouth to God's ear. When we sin, it's like adding a wad of paper in the funnel and at some point God can't hear us clearly and eventually He won't hear us at all. That has stuck with me my whole life. Not that it stopped me from sinning, but as I've matured in Christ, I try to sin less, and I do a lot of repenting.

> *Indeed, the Lord's arm is not too weak to save, and his ear is not too deaf to hear.* ² *But your iniquities are separating you from your God, and your sins have hidden his face from you so that he does not listen.*
>
> Isaiah 59:1-2 (CEB)

I will share that for me, because I know better, when I have un-married sex, I do repent, then I feel bad. Not only that, but there have also been instances where that act has cost me, and I felt that I paid for it in other ways. When I was entering into temptation, I've always had that nudge, poke or felt a little tug in my spirit that said don't do it, right as I was about to go into the act, but I was in the throes of passion, and I didn't (or I should say my body didn't) want to stop. I knew right then and there that I was being disobedient, but I didn't care.

Well God cared and very soon thereafter in one instance I went to start my car as I did any other day, pulled into the main street and my battery died. Well after the tow to the dealership, they kept my car for 3 weeks. $2000 later, less Uber expenses, what could I say, I knew I shouldn't have sinned when God was trying to warn me.

No temptation has overtaken you except what is common to mankind. And God is faithful; he will not let you be tempted beyond what you can bear. But when you are tempted, he will also provide a way out so that you can endure it.

1 Corinthians 10:13 (NIV)

This may not happen to everyone. God deals with each person differently. I truly believe it really depends on where you are in your walk with Christ and what He is trying to do in your life. God loves us all and I love you enough to be transparent.

SOUL TIES

The second thing that happens when you are unmarried and having sex is having to deal with ungodly soul ties. Soul ties are what binds you and your sex partner's souls and emotions together. This is perfect if it is with your husband, but if you are either sleeping with someone who you don't have covenant with, sleeping around with random men, or having sex with someone who is not your husband, you will end up taking on their traits, personality, dysfunctions, baggage and so on. Trust me, this is real and no joke. Most people do not deal with the adverse effects of soul-ties until things go south.

Now as a woman, I know what some of you may be thinking; I want his soul tied to mine so that he won't leave, cheat, and will stay connected to me or even better, he'll commit to me. But a soul tie has nothing to do with personalities. If your partner wanted to cheat or disrespect you, a soul tie doesn't stop them from doing those things, and it doesn't entice someone to be with you. But soul-ties are spiritual and can make it harder for you to walk away or detach. That's why you can have the best sex ever with a man, but still not be compatible. Same with a man, you can give him the best sex ever, but that doesn't mean he'll be faithful. But you must be aware that all of the people your partner slept with, their spirits are competing with yours and that alone can be a root cause of any rifts you are having in the relationship and not understand why. I'd encourage you to read the story about the woman and the well when God told her she had many husbands, and she was not legally married. Who was he referring to when He told her to go and call her husband?

> *"I have no husband," she replied. Jesus said to her, "You are right when you say you have no husband. [18] The fact is, you have had five husbands, and the man you now have is not your husband. What you have just said is quite true."*
>
> *John 4:17-18*

I recall when I first discovered soul ties, I was in a situationship and found myself thinking of that person non-stop, having lustful thoughts of them, upset if I couldn't see them, and feeling like I'd do anything to be with them. I knew it was very unhealthy for me and therefore I had to cut them off, because it was not a situation, I wanted to be in. However, I found myself feeling like I was enslaved to that person emotionally. My judgment was clouded because although I was hurt, I was still lusting after them, and considering taking them back. It was like a weird connection, although I knew I would never be in a relationship with his person, I wanted to be with them.

One day I was talking to a girlfriend of mine, describing how I was feeling, and she told me that it was a soul tie. I'd never heard of that before, but after she explained it to me, she immediately prayed with me to bind up that soul tie, claim my body parts back, repent for the sin and renounce the person in prayer and I immediately felt a release. Unfortunately, I've had to do this a few times when those feelings returned when things situations occurred like receiving a text from them.

Upon this discovery, I found myself wanting to be free from every man that I ever laid down with who was not my husband. I wanted to be delivered from people in my past and those occasional slip-ups, so I took out time to break every soul tie from everyone in my past, including all people in general that I did not have a healthy (non-sexual) relationship with.

Sometimes you don't do a full cleansing and have to go back and get in the corners, cracks, and crevices to be fully rid of that spirit. After all of that praying, put on your full armor of God and make sure there are no chinks in your armor, or any pieces missing.

Praying against un-godly soul ties is much more than repentance, you must really think about and identify all the things you've confessed with your mouth to your sex partner. If you ever recall or found yourself saying in the sex act things like they were the best you ever had, baby it's yours, take it. You know all the things you said to entice your man, stroke his ego, make him feel like a king when he was rocking your world? You have to repent for all of that and take it back.

When you make those declarations to someone who is not your spouse, you are making a spiritual covenant with them and that is not so easy to just walk away from. It takes some serious prayer, time spent on your knees, and a spiritual detox to rid your soul of those connections.

> *But he who is joined to the Lord is one spirit with Him.* [18] *Flee sexual immorality. Every sin that a man does is outside the body, but he who commits sexual immorality sins against his own body.*
>
> *1 Corinthians 6:17-18*

Here is a sample prayer of breaking ungodly soul-ties.

Heavenly Father, I cut off the evil soul tie that formed between any sexual partner who I have laid down with and have given authority over my body and mind. I declare restoration on the portions of my life and my body parts that have been used, broken, and crushed, in the name of Jesus. Heal my heart and help me to choose the right kind of relationships from this point on.

I stand firm in that authority and declare that I am free from any ungodly soul ties, in Jesus' name.

By the power, in the blood of Jesus, I break free from any covenants and agreements I made with those people in the mighty name of Jesus. I decree and declare that I am free, and those agreements are null and void from today onwards. In Jesus' name, I pray, Amen.

I'm certainly no expert, I'm just sharing with you how God dealt with me, and He did so that I can share it with you. If you love yourself, this practice is worth going back to renounce all old relationships so that your new one doesn't compete with those spirits in you.

There are many instances in the bible where God tries to warn us so that we can avoid heartache later. I love how the book of Proverbs gives such wisdom about this topic. After reading chapter 5, I literally wrote at the top of the page in my bible, "Don't be a Hoe!" As it is written, it references a woman but also applies to men. It's about avoiding seduction. Reading through the scriptures, we are warned to listen to wise counsel, stay away from people who would seduce us. You know the ones who talk a really good game? You know the one who your mind is telling you no, but your body is screaming YES! It's a trap, don't do it.

> *Keep your way far from her. Don't go near the door of her house.* [9] *Otherwise, you will give up your vitality to others and your years to someone*

> cruel; [10] *strangers will drain your resources, and your hard-earned pay will end up in a foreigner's house.* [11] *At the end of your life, you will lament when your physical body has been consumed,* [12] *and you will say, "How I hated discipline, and how my heart despised correction.* [13] *I didn't obey my teachers or listen closely to my instructors.* [14] *I am on the verge of complete ruin before the entire community."*
>
> Proverbs 5:8-14 (CSB)

And I've felt that way dealing with soul ties, but I'm determined to break out of this cycle because that feeling of ruin, distress, obsession, whatever name you give it is not worth it in the end.

There were a few instances, I have been so close to marriage, but never closed the deal. I've had men who loved me, but none love me "enough" to fight for the relationship. I compare it to a house built on a weak foundation. Think about it, you have this house, it looks good, and everything seems structurally sound. As long as conditions are good, you don't have any problems, however, once a strong wind comes or when that storm comes it will test the foundation and that foundation falls. That's how some of my relationships have been for me and that's so disappointing because you don't see it right away and of course, everything seemed great until the crash.

I pray for a man who has and can provide a solid foundation so that when a storm comes, I know we can withstand whatever comes our way. And because I've learned so many lessons, my eye is better trained to identify flaws, cracks, and an unstable foundation, and when I identify them, I'm moving out! To get with me, there has to be a house made of bricks, not sticks. Simply meaning I desire a man who won't cave under pressure, but who is able to deal with issues and work them out.

You must be willing to put yourself first and choose your happiness over a fantasy.

Let's face it the pain of heartbreak is real, but you don't want to allow it to scare you off from ever loving again. This entire process of dating, introducing someone new in your life, meshing personalities, trusting again, having disagreements is scary, but you don't have to do it alone. God's got you! Typically, the problem is us, it's not God. We don't invite Him in until there is a problem. We also tend to not want to wait for God's answer when we pray. But let's start fresh. God can meet us where we're at.

Relationships are a gift from God, but they are also hard work. The blessing is that relationships are also rewarding and should be taken seriously just as any other important thing in your life. Spending time praying, fasting, meditating is very important before and while you're in a relationship. Even if you find that you made bad choices, repent, and turn from the sin, God is faithful to forgive. God is the master, he is the potter, and He is your comforter.

It is my prayer that you have taken away some helpful pointers that will encourage you to seek God's face and His will for your life concerning relationships, commitment, and marriage. Overall, I hope that you always feel valued and understand that you deserve and can have better. God is faithful.

Bonus Content: Look for Your Blessings

Have you ever heard the story of counting yellow cars? It's a story I heard years ago as an analogy to train your mind to discover answers.

Have you ever realized that whatever you need is already inside of you? God equipped us with the Holy Spirit and His angels as tools to guide us each day, it's just a matter of tapping into those resources.

ARE YOU LISTENING?

God has given us discernment, also known in the world as intuition – it's that "gut" feeling or internal voice. That voice should never be ignored, if that muscle is weak, you must exercise it to be stronger. God will send an angel over you, and they will whisper the answer to you in your ear. God also puts people and experiences in front of us for us to learn from them both whether good or bad. The main thing is are you listening?

Have you ever stopped and asked yourself questions like "what am I doing here?" "where should I go?", "what direction should I take?" "Is this person the right person for me?"

Once you start to ask yourself questions, you can train yourself to look out or pay attention for the answers.

You'll find it almost humorous how answers are revealed. It could be very casual such as overhearing a conversation that contained the answer you needed, it could be commentary you heard while watching television that gave you the solution or random conversation- you just never know but the answers are there, but you have to look for it.

The best thing to do is pray first, get a concordance, and look up the words you are feeling and find reference scriptures. Then open your bible and see what God say's about it, you'll be amazed just how the bible holds all the answers to your questions.

Make it a habit to spend time in prayer, worshipping God, thanking Him for what He can and will do, daily read your Bible, and meditation on God's Word throughout the day. As you read God's Word, ask Him to speak to you. Wait expectantly and obey whatever God tells you to do.

YELLOW CAR CHALLENGE

I want to help you exercise that discernment muscle by doing the Yellow Car Challenge. This will test your ability to seek out what you are hoping to find. Try this challenge for 7 days. Set out to see how many yellow cars you can count in a day by first setting a number. Start with five, then go up in increments of five for 7 days.

> *When you change the way you look at things, things change the way they look.*

You must tell yourself "Today, I want to find 5 yellow cars." Watch how your mind opens and you will start to notice yellow cars. Keep track for a week.

Again, you will see how your subconsciousness mind has opened to recognize what was already there, and soon, you will start to see more and more. You will see that there wasn't an influx of yellow cars, but they had been there all along.

The same with God, His blessings are all around us, and sometimes we just have to reach up and grab them. We become so distracted and clouded and ignore the answers that have been there all along. Doing this little exercise will demonstrate how we seek God for answers and can position ourselves to see the answers that were already in front of us.

You have to be quiet in order to hear God speak". The reason why God may never speak to you could be because you're never quiet. Something is always going on in your mind, so while God is trying to get through to you on the telephone of life, he's getting a busy signal. You've got to reserve time alone with God. - Rick Warren

Don't Be a Doormat: Get Out with Your Integrity Intact

www.ingramcontent.com/pod-product-compliance
Lightning Source LLC
LaVergne TN
LVHW021408080426
835508LV00020B/2493